I wish you
two many years of
great vacations.
Much Aloha!
Jessica

MAUI

SILVERSWORD

MAUI

UPCOUNTRY MAUI

WAILEA BEACH

MAUI

Photography by **Douglas Peebles**

Text by **Jan TenBruggencate**

Mutual Publishing

Library of Congress Catalog Card Number 00-107475

Book Design by Michael Horton Design

ISBN-10: 1-56647-323-3
ISBN-13: 978-1-56647-323-1

Tenth Printing, January 2014

Mutual Publishing
1215 Center Street, Suite 210
Honolulu, Hawai'i 96816
Telephone (808) 732-1709
Fax (808) 734-4094
email: info@mutualpublishing.com
www.mutualpublishing.com
Printed in China

TABLE OF CONTENTS

PARADISE FOUND

OVER THE PAST 25 YEARS

I have probably made over a hundred trips to the islands of Maui, Molokaʻi and Lānaʻi from my home on windward Oʻahu. I have always enjoyed the islands of Maui County, but the last dozen or so trips that I made for this book have brought the reasons more into focus.

It is not just the beauty of the Island's beaches, mountains and valleys that appeals to me, it is also their diversity. It is not the same diversity as the Big Island of Hawaiʻi, where you can go from snow-capped mountain to hot lava pouring in the ocean in a few hours, or from rain forest to desert in a few minutes. On Maui, Molokaʻi, and Lānaʻi, I believe the diversity comes from the people who have chosen to come here and their reasons for doing so.

There are a lot of people searching for paradise here, and they are finding it in a number of different ways. For sailboarders it is Hoʻokipa, Māʻalaea, or Kanahā. For whale watchers it is the ʻAlalākieki Channel between the islands. For golfers there is Kapalua, Kāʻanapali, Wailea, Mākena and Lānaʻi. Divers head to Molokini or Lānaʻi among other spots. Crystal worshipers and searchers for the lost continent of Mu have their special places, as well. Beachcombers and hikers have choices too numerous to list.

My last trip was seven days of kayaking and camping down the Hāna Coast. My friend Gary Budlong found his paradise at a remote waterfall that his daughter had told him about. I found mine a couple of miles up the coast just lying in a hammock and watching the sunset.

Douglas Peebles

FOREWORD

MAUI IS KNOWN AROUND the world for beaches, fun, whale watching, diving, windsurfing, fine dining, sublime sunsets—in short, for all the activities that make a perfect visitor destination. But Maui is more.

In a time before humans entered the Polynesian region of the Pacific, a vast island stood up out of the water, full of life and great sweeping vistas. The nameless peaks filled the sky near and far.

The land ran from the edge of the sea to alpine heights, and included ranges of climate to suit every taste. Plants and birds and insects filled each niche, from closed-canopy dryland forests to dense, multilevel rain forests, from coastal dune ecosystems to scrublands above the treeline. The birdlife included birds in traditional roles, but also ones that filled all the niches in this environment that mammals did on the continents and marsupials did in Australia. There were carrion-eaters, predators and even grazing animals. Many were earth-bound, having lost their ability, along with their need, to fly.

KA'ANAPALI

HULA

This was a strange world, with creatures unlike those found anywhere else, and plants unique in the world, on a stunning island isolated near one end of a long archipelago in the center of the northern Pacific Ocean.

The island was Maui Nui, Great Maui, and it included the volcanoes that are now Kaho'olawe, East and West Maui, Lāna'i, East and West Moloka'i and a now-submerged volcano west of Moloka'i, known today as Penguin Banks.

Over the years, the level of the sea rose, filling the valleys between the volcanoes, until the peaks were isolated in ones and twos, with shallow channels between them.

KĀʻANAPALI

Humans came in wooden canoes, and later in planked boats, and then steel ships and, finally, aluminum aircraft. The islands of Maui Nui became Maui County—different, but still among the most enchanting places on the planet.

BANANA

Because of their prehistoric connection, many of the plant species on one island of this group are much more like each other than they are like those on other Hawaiian islands. The birds, and the insects and the tree snails, too, are this way.

KAUPŌ RANCH

There are spots on each of the islands of the group from which you can see all the others. Places on West Maui, East Moloka'i, South Lāna'i, and Northeast Kaho'olawe provide vistas that give a sense of the size of the old Maui Nui. The channels between the islands are narrow, but can be treacherous. Ships have been lost and sailors and swimmers swept away by the winds whipping between the mountains and the currents surging through the channels. Maui Nui was one, but now is distinctly four. Each island has its own flavor, its own character. And, in a sense, each mountain is unique.

Their elevations and situation with respect to the trade wind flow also provide the islands with individual characteristics. For instance, low West Moloka'i in appearance is like Kaho'olawe and much of Lāna'i, as none has the elevation to trap the trade wind showers. East Moloka'i recalls West Maui for its rugged, deep-cut valleys, eroded by rainfall. The

4

wild, wet Hāna coastline is much like the north shore valleys of Moloka'i, with a wild profusion of greenery over a jagged, rocky topography.

These are islands that generate strong feelings of belonging among their residents. And they have attracted visitors for hundreds of years. For better or for worse, each new wave of visitors has brought change. The early Polynesian settlers transformed the lowlands, using fire and farming and sheer expanding numbers to convert the original terrain to their own uses. Whalers brought their own economy, creating rowdy towns and a taste in the population for the uses of cash. Sandalwood traders promoted the rape of the fragrant woods of the Hawaiian forests. Sugar farmers diverted streams and made dry lands fertile. Pineapple growers

MOLOKINI

HUMPBACK WHALE POD

brought their golden-fruited crop to drier lands often unsuitable for sugar. And eventually came tourism, which brought roads and buildings to isolated beaches whose value no one in the agricultural age had anticipated.

Except that in Maui County, not every beach was for sale. East Moloka'i, for instance, maintains strict controls on development. Kaho'olawe, once a sheep ranch and then a bombing target, is now being converted into a cultural icon of the Hawaiian people. The Hāna coastline is so rugged that few resorts have been able to find a foothold. And the one corporation that owns almost all of Lāna'i has placed only a single resort on the shore, leaving miles of sandy beach to residents and adventurous tourists.

Maui County is an eclectic mix of places and peoples and cultures. It is home to the super-rich and ultra-sophisticated. And back-to-the-land types in organic cotton trousers, batik shirts and hemp bags. And Native Hawaiians who want to re-establish a sovereign Hawaiian nation. And cowboys, and techies, and hula girls, and surfers, and dirt farmers, and bureaucrats.

HĀNA COAST

It is a place where cutting-edge science and technology is performed, with a supercomputer in the lowlands and space telescopes atop the summit of its highest mountain, Haleakalā. And it's a place that helped develop the sport of windsurfing.

HĀNA

Fine Hawaiian coffee is grown here, and the famed sweet Maui onions, and the spiky brilliant protea flowers.

KAUNAKAKAI HARBOR

And then there is the visitor industry. The Maui visitor indiustry is be one of the most sophisticated in the world. It attracts the top entertainers, top chefs, top convention speakers. Maui offers virtually every water activity a sun-drenched visitor could ask for.

There are even off the ocean activities, like swimming in chill mountain pools, under misting waterfalls. But most are by and of the

HĀNA

sea. Parasail high over the pale blue nearshore waters, dive the coral reefs of an offshore island, sail to an isolated beach, fish in the channels between the islands, or watch whales watching you watching them.

The smaller islands offer activities that tend to be more country. Horseback riding or mountain biking on Moloka'i, for example. Or four-wheeling the dusty back roads of Lāna'i. An invitation to Kaho'olawe is unlikely in the near term, since the cleanup of the island after a generation of military activities is expected to take a while. But, if you were to visit, the food would be simple and the activities supportive of the effort to revive the island"s environment.

The environment is what Maui County is known for. It is what keeps its residents here and brings visitors, back year after year.

HĀNA

7

KĀʻANAPALI

WAIKANI FALLS, A.K.A. THREE BEARS

WEST MAUI

THE HEART OF

West Maui is the tourist town of Lahaina, whose name refers to the fine weather of this part of the island. It can be translated the "merciless sun". Perfect for tourism. The calm weather also makes for a nice anchorage, one of the reasons it was a home of royalty, a whaling port, and the Hawaiian nation's first capital.

KĀʻANAPALI

A replica whaler, the steel-hulled *Carthaginian II*, was anchored for three decades at Lahaina as a floating museum memorializing the island's whaling history. In 2005, the aged ship was sunk in 95 feet of water a half-mile off Lahaina. It now serves as a living reef and is visited by scuba divers and submarine tours.

Lahaina is a town with history. Today, you can find fragments of that history scattered through the town. Note the mined coral blocks that form the old prison and the missionary home that is the oldest coral block house in Hawaiʻi. These building blocks were in common use during the first half of the 1800s. Whalers, missionaries and Hawaiian kings were brought together in the ferment of this period in Lahaina. The town also has the reputation of being the immigration point for the first mosquitoes brought to the Islands. They are believed to have arrived in the water casks of the sailing ship *Wellington*, which arrived at Lahaina in 1826 on a voyage from Mexico.

NAPILI BAY

Note the architecture of the Pioneer Inn, which dates to the turn of the last century. The old sugar mill in town is a reminder of a more recent economic history, but Lahaina's sugar days ended with the end of the 1900s. The mill site

FRONT STREET, LAHAINA

dates to 1860. Down Front Street, there are buildings that are old or made to look old, all of them an active part of the new economic machine—tourism. Off the beach, you can see more of the impact of tourism, as visitors soar high over the sea under parasails, and ride the boats into the habitat of the humpback whales in winter, dive the beaches, take fishing charters and sail the scenic coast.

WO HING MUSEUM

But West Maui is more than Lahaina. It begins with a drive along the coast from the isthmus that connects this mountain mass with the larger body of Haleakalā. The highway drops from coastal cliffs and slides through the quiet flats surrounding Olowalu, along miles of beach. Beyond Lahaina are resort complexes that include Kā'anapali, named after a rock cliff here, and Honokōwai, whose name recalls the movement of plumes of fresh water in the salty bay, and Kahana, Nāpili and Kapalua. Farther around this end of the island is the scenic bay of Honokōhau and

NORFOLK PINE TREES, KAPALUA

NAPILI BAY

the quiet fishing and taro-growing village of Kahakuloa, windows into the Hawaiʻi lifestyle two centuries past.

West Maui has the further feature of being in the middle of old Maui Nui. From here, you can see Molokaʻi to the west and north, Lānaʻi to the west and south, Kahoʻolawe to the southeast and Haleakalā to the east. From this part of Maui, you have the sense of being among islands. Most of the state's other resort areas look out onto open ocean.

KĀʻANAPALI

Many residents never get beyond the coast and the ocean, but, upslope, there is a great deal more. At Lahaina, annual rainfall averages 14 inches. Up the hill at *Puʻu Kukui*, the top of the West Maui volcano, the driest month of the year has a higher average rainfall. The more than 400 inches of rain at the top of the mountain helped support agriculture on the arid south and west-facing coastline below. Water diverted from streams irrigated sugar cane for a century and a half. Now it grows other varieties of grass: condominium lawns and golf course greens. Landowners in recent years have banded together to protect the upland forest of this region, since a dense native forest is a far better watershed than one eroded by pig and grazing animal damage or dominated by a single-species of alien weedy plants.

The wind and, with it, the rain transform the northeast side of West Maui. Aside from the hamlet of Honokōhau and the village of Kahakuloa, it is a mostly unpopulated countryside of steep valleys and rugged cliffs. While the climate of the southwest side is calm and sunny, the northeast side is where trade winds batter the vegetation, and North Pacific storms pound the rocky coastline.

LAHAINA HARBOR

KAPALUA

LAHAINA BANYAN TREE

BELLSTONE TIDE POOLS

HONOLUA BAY

KĀʻANAPALI

LAHAINA

KAHAKULOA
Previous pages

KAHAKULOA

FRONT STREET, LAHAINA

CENTRAL MAUI

THE GREAT CENTRAL

valley of Maui is the island's agricultural wonderpiece. Here flows the water from an immense irrigation system, with 84 miles of ditches and tunnels that drain the windward East Maui watersheds. It has been diverted to an otherwise dry countryside to create one of Hawai'i's largest sugar plantations, and one of only a handful that have survived into the 21st century. Alexander & Baldwin's Hawaiian Commercial and Sugar Co. grows all the remaining sugar cane on the island in this region. Its 37,000 acres produce 200,000 tons of raw sugar each year.

PĀ'IA TOWN

Central Maui is the working-class heart of the island. Sugar and government workers reside in the old town of Wailuku, the island's capital. The town takes its name from the river that flows to the sea here.

A narrow, deep valley on the western side of Kahului is 'Īao, whose most famous feature is a narrow ridgetop that looks like a spire. It is called 'Īao Needle. The 'Īao Valley State Park at the base of the peak provides viewers with a lush

'ĪAO VALLEY

and unusually accessible example of a windward Hawaiian valley. Here was the site of a massive battle in 1790 between the forces of Big Island chief Kamehameha, who was on a mission of conquest, and an army of the chief of Maui and O'ahu, Kahekili. Kahekili's army was led by his son, Kalanikupule. He defended a position in 'Īao Valley as Kamehameha attacked from below. While accounts suggest the armies were evenly matched, Kamehameha had a special advantage, a cannon named Lopaka, with which he pounded the enemy forces. Maui's chiefs

KANAHĀ BEACH PARK

escaped up the cliffs and valleys, but commoners were killed in such numbers that their bodies dammed the river, giving an area here the name Kepaniwai, "the damming of the waters". There is a park here that carries the name.

Next door is the newer town of Kahului, built around plantation subdivisions, with the commercial center of the island at its seaward edge. The Kahului Harbor is the island's primary commercial harbor. It's where barges bring in all of Maui's staples. Next in line, heading east, is Maui's main airport, which accommodates flights from the other islands and from across the sea. One of the major political issues of the past decade has been the battle over whether to allow the expansion of the airport runway to bring in even more and larger jets from abroad.

While little of the original wildlife of this region has survived the commercialization and farming of the area, there is a special little spot nestled between the shopping centers of Kahului and the airport. It is Kanahā Pond, a wildlife refuge frequented by the endangered Hawaiian stilt and a range of migratory waterbirds.

HO'OKIPA

KANAHA BEACH

MAUI OCEAN CENTER

The town of Pā'ia was built on the sugar industry but has evolved into a cute tourist stopping place. Its storefronts house fewer residential staples, those now being provided primarily by the shopping centers in Kahului. Instead, Pā'ia is a colorful town of art shops, surfing culture, eateries and snack food places. Uphill is the old sugar mill that helped the town get started. Turn east on the road to Hāna, and you shortly come to the Ho'okipa Beach Park, which has evolved into one of the state's top surfing spots. In the mornings and when the wind is down, board surfers reign here. If the wind is blowing hard, the beach and the waves burst into color with the dozens of bright windsurfing sails, dipping and flashing as their riders tack, drive and soar off the waves.

PĀ'IA

'ĪAO VALLEY

HO‘OKIPA BEACH

‘ĪAO NEEDLE
Previous pages

SUGAR CANE FIELDS

CANE FIRE

PAʻUWELA POINT
Following pages

MAUI SWAP MEET

FIRST FRIDAY FESTIVAL, WAILUKU

PĀʻIA

BANYAN TREE AT PĀʻIA SUGAR MILL
Previous pages

ORCHIDS

MOUNTAIN APPLE

BREADFRUIT

‘ĪAO NEEDLE

TORCH GINGER

THE GREAT CRESCENT

Chapter Three

UPCOUNTRY

of the south and west slopes of Haleakalā form the region that residents call Upcountry. "Up" because it's higher than most of the other residential and agricultural lands on the island, and "up" because no matter how high on the slope you go, it seems there's still more high country above you.

Clouds frequently settle down from the summit to obscure this region, whose heart is called Kula. The name means "open country", sometimes distinguished from wetlands, where *kalo*, or taro, could be grown.

PIGTAIL ANTHURIUM

Today, aside from being a bucolic residential area with cool nights and stunning views across the Maui isthmus and out to the islands beyond, the region is the center for the island's ranching and small-scale farming activities.

Carnations were once the hallmark of the Kula flower growers, but now the varied and stunning varieties of protea have largely taken their place. These tree-grown flowers are shipped around the world to form spectacular centerpieces for floral arrangements.

Small vegetable farms grow a variety of crops, of which the most famous is the Maui onion, sometimes known as the Kula onion, a sweet onion without the sharp bite of traditional onions. They are refreshing raw and, when pickled, Maui onions are a special treat.

Out near 'Ulupalakua Ranch on the south end of Upcountry Maui, vineyards flow off the slopes at an elevation of about 2,000 feet. These are modern plantings, centered around Carnelian grapes planted a generation ago by winemaker

CHURCH OF THE HOLY GHOST

HALEAKALĀ

Emil Tedeschi on Pardee Erdman's ranch lands. The winery also produces wines from pineapple and passion fruit. Winemaking has a tradition in Hawai'i that dates back more than a century. At its height, it was a homegrown business of Portuguese immigrants who produced beverages from Isabella grapes.

Cattle ranches here date to the 1800s, and the town of Makawao is a combination of tourist chic and old cowboy town, recalling in its architecture a legitimate ranching background.

Kula has a range of small towns and neighborhoods, many shaded by jacaranda and eucalyptus trees, fields of weedy black wattle and fine fruit trees.

From the heart of the Kula district, a steep road rises to the summit of Haleakalā, which every tourist guide will remind you means "house of the sun". Viewed from Kula, the sun rises from behind the volcano's upper rim. It is the place where the Hawaiian demigod Maui captured the sun and kept it tied up until it agreed to move more slowly across the skies, lengthening the Hawaiian day.

UPCOUNTRY

MAKAWAO

There is a small science complex at the 10,023-foot summit, where observatories above much of the Earth's atmosphere scan the heavens. Haleakalā is also a national park and one of the natural jewels of the state.

T. KODAMA
STORE

The great mountain creates its own weather. The moist trade winds striking the northeast slopes are driven nearly two miles upward. As they cool, the moisture condenses out of them, and rains down on a wet forest that contains unique Hawaiian plants and animals, many only recently discovered. Many species, particularly insects, remain undiscovered, scientists say.

A large portion of the eastern end of the Haleakalā National Park, the Kīpahulu Valley Biological Reserve, is closed to entry to protect its biological diversity.

HALEAKALĀ

Wildlife scientists are working constantly to protect the natural resources of the island. One major effort has been the fencing of the most important biological areas to keep out goats that eat native plants, and feral pigs, which dig up the forest floor, creating both open areas where weeds can become established and mudholes that support mosquitoes. Mosquitoes carry avian malaria and pox, which are blamed in part for the decline in Hawaiian native birdlife.

By the time the winds rise to the top of the mountain, they are largely squeezed dry.

Much of Haleakalā's summit region is barren, both because of the lack of rainfall and because what little rain that does fall quickly sinks into the porous cinder that covers much of the upper portion of the mountain.

The vast crater looks like a place on a distant planet: rocky, spotted with cindercones, alien.

On the south slopes of the mountain, the country is largely grassland and remnants of native dryland forest. Yet, there is evidence that early Hawaiians lived here. Without much rain, and without running streams, what did they do for water? One suggestion is that they collected the morning dew in calabashes, obtaining just enough moisture for survival.

MAKAWAO

ULUPALAKUA

UPCOUNTRY MAUI

HALEAKALĀ SUNRISE
Previous pages

JACARANDA TREES, ROAD TO HALEAKALĀ

SILVERSWORD

OLINDA

HALEAKALĀ

HALEAKALĀ SUNRISE

NOT TOO MANY YEARS

SOUTH COAST

ago, the Kīhei coastline was a wasteland. It was hot, covered with scrub vegetation and thorny *kiawe*, waterless. A few families had beach houses here, but hardly anyone visited the area on a regular basis. Today, people have concluded that reliable daytime sunny weather, white-sand beaches and calm water with whales breaching offshore are a perfect recipe for attracting visitors. That, along with golf, good restaurants and condominium apartment rooms with views. The wasteland has been transformed into just what many visitors to the Islands are looking for.

The South Coast is roughly spread between the little harbor at Māʻalaea to the north and La Perouse Bay to the south. The whole coastline faces the setting sun, and looks out at the islands of Lānaʻi and Kahoʻolawe, as well as the little crescent of cinder, Molokini. The ocean channel between Lānaʻi and Kahoʻolawe is called *Kealaikahiki*. Translated, this means "the way to the south" or "the way to Tahiti", suggesting it was the beginning of the favored sailing route to the ancestral home of the Native Hawaiian people in the Polynesian islands south of the equator. The

KAMAOLE BEACH

Hawaiian voyaging canoe *Hōkūleʻa* has revived some of the old routes with heroic sails to the Marquesas, Tahiti, Rapa Nui or Easter Island, and other groups throughout the region.

The strand between Māʻalaea and Keālia Pond is commonly called Sugar Beach or Māʻalaea Beach. It is long, wide and great for walking and watching wildlife. In the crescent of coastline that is formed as the south end of West Maui turns to the west side of Haleakalā is a vast flatland, often flooded, that has been preserved for wildlife. It gets its name from the salt crust that forms on the plain when the sun dries up the brackish ponds. The Keālia Pond covers 250 acres when it's wet, and far less when it's dry. It is part of the U.S. Fish and Wildlife Services complex of national wildlife refuges. Endangered hawksbill turtles nest here. A visitor may see a range of interesting birdlife, from the Pacific golden plovers that winter in Hawai'i from their nesting grounds in Alaska, to the Hawaiian stilt, a black and white wading bird with incredibly long red legs.

KEAWALA'I CHURCH (1832), MĀKENA

An ample supply of beach parks is sprinkled down the coast, a testament to Maui county's recognition that the development of the region would require public recreational facilities. Many have names that it will take visitors several trips to master, like Maipoina'oeia'u (don't forget me), Ka'ono'ulu (hungry for breadfruit), Kama'ole (childless), and Keawakapu (forbidden harbor). Some planners argue that the development of this coast was haphazard, sprawled and minimally functional, but it seems to have put many people right on the coast, which was where they want to be. Today, residential communities are building up *mauka* or inland of the coastal sweep of condos, hotels, small shopping malls, and the rest.

Down toward the southern end, the Mākena-La Perouse end, of this strip is the Wailea region, where large luxury hotels reign, along with 54 holes of golf. The shore here was recently named the best beach in America by Dr. Beach, Stephen Leatherman, who annually rates the top beaches in the country.

SUNSET, KAMA'OLE BEACH PARK

Mākena was once popular and hard to get to. Now it's popular and easier of access. Oneloa, which can be translated to "long sand", is popularly known as Big Beach. Pu'uōla'i is the name of the prominent cindercone that forms a point along this coastline. It is also the name of a small beach nearby that's known as Little Beach. The Hawaiian name of the area is commonly translated to "earthquake hill", but may also refer to the porous rock that covers the surface here. *Ōla'i* means both earthquake and pumice.

After all these Hawaiian names, it's odd to come across a clearly European one. Just south of the state's 'Āhihi-Kīna'u Natural Area Reserve lies La Perouse Bay. It is named after the French explorer who coasted along these shores in 1786, within a decade of Capt. James Cook's arrival in the Islands. The bay's little-known Hawaiian name is Keone'ō'io, or "bonefish sands", presumably a reference to the good fishing here for this species. Several bays in this region are marine preserves, preventing fishing, but ensuring excellent snorkeling when waters are calm.

Molokini Islet, off the South Maui coast, is a tuff cone, a cinder crescent that protects a stunning coral reef in the old cones basin. It is a favored spot for dive tours, which leave regularly from the harbors of South and West Maui.

KAMA'OLE BEACH PARK

'ALALĀKEIKI CHANNEL

BIG BEACH, MĀKENA

WAILEA GOLF COURSE

MAIPOINAʻOEIʻAU

KIHEI

WAILEA GOLF COURSE

MOLOKINI

MALU'AKA BEACH

WAILEA BEACH
Previous pages

WAILEA SANDCASTLE

KANAHENA AT ʻĀHIHI BAY

KEĀLIA WETLANDS
Previous pages

PA'AKO BEACH

WAILEA SUNSET

HĀNA COAST

YOU DRIFT INTO a different world as you take the road to Hāna. It's a place of greenery, few people, twisting roads and water features that would make Hollywood proud. More than four dozen bridges cross the myriad of streams that slice through this fairy landscape. It's the wet side, where the trade winds drop their loads of moisture carried across the North Pacific. Here is where sugar planters came more than a century ago for the water to irrigate Central Maui's sugar fields, using ditches and tunnels to dewater one stream after another and carry it around the flank of Haleakalā to the dry side of the island.

The Native Hawaiian communities, before the coming of other cultures, engineered water systems here far earlier. Tiny communities of the windward East Maui coastline are generally built around the old taro fields, where the ancient crop grows in ponds hundreds of years old. The crops are flooded with flowing, not standing, water.

After Huelo and Kailua, the gateways to the Hāna road, the primary communities of the wettest part of the region are Ke'anae, Wailua and Nāhiku, which is home to the immense Pi'ilanihale Heiau, a 500-year-old Hawaiian temple with massive stone walls. It is believed to be the largest single heiau in all of Hawai'i.

SHAVE ICE

Today, the Hāna coastline is a kind of rural backwater, in part because of its difficulty of access, but also because many people today prefer sunnier weather. But in the early days of human activities here, it was an important place. Even in the narrow gullies, the availability of water made the place an agricultural mecca, with taro the central crop. The ocean is often rough here, but the coastal communities augmented the land's crops with

MAKALIKO RODEO

MANGOS AND
STARFRUITS

fish, pushing canoes out to sea to jig for bottom fish, troll for tuna and surround congregations of the schooling fish, 'ōpelu and akule.

Nearer the village of Hāna, the Wai'ānapanapa State Park features a scenic rocky shoreline and the stunning semi-submerged caves from whose shining waters the area gets its name. One of the caves is reached by swimming from another through an underwater passage.

The urban center of the Hāna coast is the town of that name, where some 2,000 people live in a community built on the slopes behind a small bay. The region has developed into a retreat for the wealthy and a place where many local residents feel that a piece of old Hawai'i still survives.

In the years when canoes were the primary form of transport, Hāna was an important spot because it was one of the first places a fleet of canoes could readily come ashore when sailing from the Big Island. When the chief Piha-a-Pi'ilani sailed to make war on his older brother, Maui ruler Lono-a-Pi'ilani, he sailed first to Hāna. Hāna was too well defended, so he redirected the fleet to Wailua, and ultimately conquered the island.

HĀMOA BEACH

A few generations later, the Hawai'i chief Kalaniōpu'u launched a war and annexed Hāna to his Big Island's holdings. Control over the region as the years progressed went back and forth between Maui and Big Island chiefs. In 1790, Kamehameha settled things. He landed a fleet from the Big Island

HĀNA

so large that to beach the canoes it required all the shores from Hāmoa to Kawaipapa, nearly four miles of coastline. The subsequent battle between Kamehameha's forces and those of Maui was named Kawa'anui, "the many canoe"s. One of the boats even carried a cannon, handled by Kamehameha's Western chiefs, John Young and Isaac Davis. The invasion eventually led to the 'Īao Valley battle in which the cannon, Lopaka, was decisive.

The island's coastline turns in the region of Hāna town from one facing the northeast trade winds to one lying protected from them. As a result, the climate and the countryside are drier as you bounce and turn toward the west.

Beyond Hāna, the little white-sand beach of Hāmoa is one of the prettiest in the Islands, and farther along is the eastern end of the Haleakalā National Park, where the many pools of 'Ohe'o Gulch, once called the Seven Sacred Pools, step down toward the sea. There aren't just seven pools. Depending on where you stop counting, you can easily count past twenty. Next comes Kīpahulu. Shortly, along this route, the road turns to dirt and rock, and can be treacherous for two-wheel-drive passenger vehicles. In heavy rainfall, it is sometimes washed out. If you are able to stay with it, it cruises past quiet Kaupō through the drylands of leeward Haleakalā and eventually rises to 'Ulupalakua and Kula.

'OHE'O GULCH

ROAD TO HĀNA

PUKAULUA POINT
Previous pages

WAILUA FALLS

WAI'ĀNAPANAPA STATE PARK

KE'ANAE VALLEY

ROAD TO HĀNA

MANAWAINUI VALLEY

KE'ANAE PENINSULA
Previous pages

PAUWALU POINT

MOLOKA'I

THE LONG ISLAND

of Moloka'i has worn many faces.

It has been described as a cowboy island, though in recent years the working cattle operations are taking a back seat to the dude ranch tourism ventures of its biggest landowner, Molokai Ranch.

It was a pineapple island, but the fields of these bromeliad relatives have reverted to pasture and other crops. The crops of watermelons, basil, coffee and sometimes onions and potatoes now spread around the Ho'olehua area near the island's airport were once all pineapple.

PLUMERIA

In early Hawai'i it was known as Moloka'i pule o'o, or "Moloka'i of the powerful prayer". It was a land of skilled Hawaiian priests and sorcerers, the most notable of whom was Lanikaula. This slayer of mythical lizard monsters was eventually killed through sorcery himself. He was buried in a grove of *kukui* trees, the symbol trees of the island, on the far east end of Moloka'i. Local tradition suggests that even today, centuries later, his power persists and it is dangerous to enter the grove, whose name is Ulu-kukui-o-Lanikaula, "the *kukui* grove of Lanikaula".

HĀKA'A'ANO

HULA PIKO

In legend, this island was the home of Hina, the mother of the demigod Maui. The island's signature song recalls this connection: Moloka'i nui a Hina. Today, fealty to traditional gods is supplanted by a new religion, represented in part by a row of Christian churches, across the highway from the 140-year-old Kapuāiwa coconut grove west of Kaunakakai.

While the island's modern spelling includes the glottal stop marker, known in Hawaiian as an ʻokina or ʻuʻina, some old-timers insist that this is incorrect, and that the original pronunciation of the word gave it just three syllables, Molo, meaning twisted, and kai, meaning sea, perhaps a reference to the ocean currents that sweep around the island. Today's primary reference on the subject, the book *Place Names of Hawaiʻi*, uses Molokaʻi, thus so will this volume.

The low Makanalua peninsula, which juts out at the base of high cliffs on the northern side of the island, was set aside as a place of isolation for those who suffered from Hansen's disease, or leprosy. The village here, Kalaupapa, is still home to a few elderly patients, although the disease is now entirely controlled by modern medicine. The area is under the joint control of the State Department of Health and the National Park Service, which manages it as a National Historical Park.

MOLOKAʻI

One of the earliest known Polynesian settlements was at Hālawa on the eastern end of the island, where Hawaiian chiefs gathered to ride the surf. Young people still surf the Hālawa break today.

The great coastal reef plain that runs along almost the whole south side of the island supports the remains of the largest surviving collection of Hawaiian fishponds, evidence of an active aquaculture industry in the pre-contact period. Some of the ponds are being revived, supporting crops of seaweeds and fishes like mullet.

MOLOKAʻI MULE RIDE

There was a Hawaiian school of navigation and astronomy on the highlands near Kalaʻe.

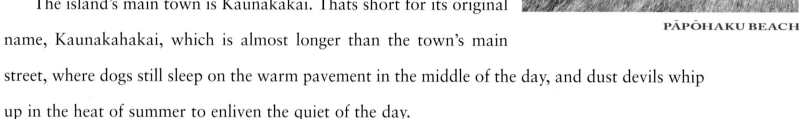

PĀPŌHAKU BEACH

Today, the Kalaʻe region is best known as the site of a mule ride down to Kalaupapa, and site of perhaps the most sexually explicit stone in the world, the famous Phallic Rock, Kauleonānāhoa.

The island's main town is Kaunakakai. Thats short for its original

MOLOKAʻI MULE RIDE

name, Kaunakahakai, which is almost longer than the town's main street, where dogs still sleep on the warm pavement in the middle of the day, and dust devils whip up in the heat of summer to enliven the quiet of the day.

Molokaʻi is made up of two volcanoes. The lower western mountain reaches only 1,381 feet and catches little rainfall. It is noted for its sunny, dry climate. The eastern side, with its peak at Kamakou, is almost a mile high at 4,970 feet. It supports a rain forest that is protected by The Nature Conservancy of Hawaiʻi, which is working to control fire, pigs, weedy plants, rats and other threats in its efforts to preserve a remarkable, complex Hawaiian wet forest ecosystem and a crucial watershed on an island whose water supplies are limited.

The Hawaiian Homes Commission Act of 1920, which provided land for homesteads for Native Hawaiians, had its first successes on Molokaʻi, when homesteaders turned the Kalamaʻula area, outside Kaunakakai, into a green Eden. It had its first failure a few years later when the shallow freshwater lens was exhausted, and Kalamaʻula's wells turned salty. Today, access to water for drinking and irrigation remains one of the hot political issues of the island.

HULA

KAPUĀIWA COCONUT GROVE

MOʻOMOMI DUNES

MOAʻULA FALLS

KAINALU

HUELO ISLET

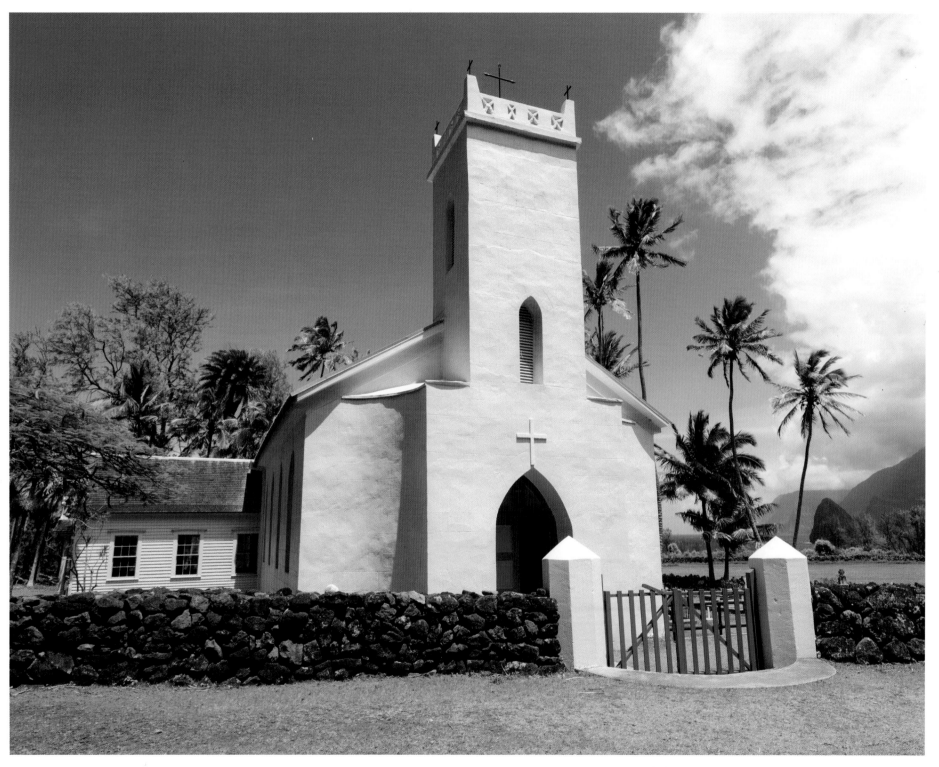

ST. PHILOMENA CHURCH

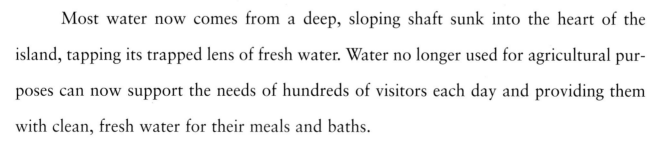

KAUNOLU

Chapter Seven

LĀNA'I

THE ISLAND IN THE

lee of the 'Au'au Channel, Lāna'i is a short boat ride from Maui or Moloka'i. Tour vessels daily cross the waters for picnics at a small park-like parcel on the northeast shore, where a dock reaches out onto the reef. This area, however, is green only because most of the vegetation planted here are salt-tolerant. Good fresh water was so rare in the early days then, when one village had a well producing good water, such as the one at Kaunolū, other people from neighboring villages would come to use it. Lāna'i is a dry island. It has no running streams, and wells dug on its eroded northern flats generate brackish water. It is why efforts at large-scale agriculture here, such as the *Maunalei* Sugar Company, failed. The products that have done well on the island are pineapple and tourism, and pineapple is gone, the result of a business decision by the island's owners to emphasize tourism and to convert the island's working population from farmers to landscapers, bellhops, room service workers and other occupations that support the visitor experience.

GARDEN OF THE GODS

Most water now comes from a deep, sloping shaft sunk into the heart of the island, tapping its trapped lens of fresh water. Water no longer used for agricultural purposes can now support the needs of hundreds of visitors each day and providing them with clean, fresh water for their meals and baths.

Visitors to the island can easily spend their entire time at and around their hotels, each of which is unique, missing the natural wonders of the island.

POLIHUA BEACH

The Lodge at Kō'ele, on the outskirts of Lāna'i City, is an unusual resort in Hawai'i. It's first class, and it's well off any beach. The design is a little English country estate, a little Hawai'i upland, with a Greg Norman golf course and a collection of ponds and a glass orchid house tossed in. The Lodge is one of Hawai'i's premier resorts.

Just across town is the original island hotel, the 10-room Hotel Lāna'i, a 1923 guest house set among the Norfolk Island pines for which this island's only town is famous. These towering trees, which are not true pines, were planted in an attempt to improve the climate and appearance of Lāna'i City. The Hotel Lāna'i is modest, quiet and more a part of the community than the two big resorts.

The island's traditional coastal resort is the Manele Bay Hotel, overlooking one of the prettiest bays in all Hawai'i, Hulopo'e. The resort's green tile-roofed buildings tumble toward the shore from irrigated green lawns. Guests have the option of swimming in the ocean or a freshwater pool. The white-sand beach of the bay, the islands most popular swimming beach and a site for residents' family picnics and campers, is Lāna'i's chief mixing place. Most of this island's roads are dirt; in dry weather they are dust, and in wet weather they are mud, although there isn't much wet weather on Lāna'i. That's why this is the only island where four-wheel-drive rental cars are common.

MANELE BAY HOTEL

It is an island for exploring, though it is difficult to get lost. Virtually all roads on the island lead out from the center, like spokes on a wheel. The easiest scenic drive is the paved road that crosses the center ridge down to the north side of the island, and then the flat sand and dust road

LUAHIWA PETROGLYPHS

SHIPWRECK BEACH

that runs along a coastline of white and gray-sand beaches, with views of Moloka'i, Maui and Kaho'olawe. The wind that sweeps through the Pailolo Channel between Moloka'i and Maui can blast this coastline, but the extensive reefs protect the shore.

A summit road takes four-wheel-drivers and hikers over the 3,370-foot highest part of the island, Lāna'ihale, and through the tiny patch of rain forest there.

Another road bounces through the eroded rock formations of Garden of the Gods and down to Polihua Beach, where sea turtles come ashore to lay their eggs. One Hawaiian tradition holds that a god of the sea created the first turtle on this beach.

A cliff coastline runs from this area around the southwest side to the island's only harbor at Kaumalapau. Between Kaumalapau and the Manele Bay Hotel, the old Hawaiian fishing village of Kaunolū sits on the southernmost point of the island. The drive down a rock and dirt road is very challenging. A self-guided tour displays a range of house and temple sites, including a home where Kamehameha the Great stayed when he visited this spot.

HULUPO‘E

LĀNA‘I CITY
Following pages 125

KAHO'OLAWE

THE DRIEST OF THE eight major islands of Hawai'i might have seemed an unlikely candidate for being the spark of the renaissance of Hawaiian culture, but Kaho'olawe played a major role. Young Hawaiians of the 1970s fought hard to extract the island from the control of the U.S. Navy, which used it as a bombing target. They employed techniques ranging from lobbying Congress to staging protest occupations of the island, with members of the Kaho'olawe 'Ohana sometimes hiding out on the island to thwart Navy search teams.

The effort to extract the island from military control was ultimately successful, and the bombing was stopped in 1990. The federal government is now funding a program to clear Kaho'olawe of unexploded munitions and to replant eroded areas, largely in native plants.

The place is very dry, since it is a low island lying in the lee of Maui. Rain clouds often lose their moisture over the taller Maui mountains, and pass high over Kaho'olawe's 1,477-foot peak, Lua Makika, without ever slowing to share their moisture.

The island once was covered by a native dryland forest, but even then was arid. One Hawaiian saying refers to the island as "one that eats foods only eaten during times of famine". Another refers to the clouds of dust raised from the island when the trade wind blows.

The island is 11 miles long and 8 miles wide, and no point is more than 2.4 miles from the sea. It has no permanent running stream. There is ample archaeological evidence that early residents of the Islands used Kaho'olawe, but the parched conditions suggest that for most people, the use may have been seasonal, as was the case for several of the driest spots in the Islands. In early days, it was politically linked to Maui, and was probably inhabited

KAHO‘OLAWE

by no more than a few hundred people, probably primarily as a fishing site, a place for wet season dryland agriculture. Residents probably used standing water from temporary pools left after rains, and also water from springs and shallow wells. It is near enough to Maui that it would have been easily possible to paddle or sail a canoe to Maui to get an emergency water supply and to return within the same day, or even the same morning.

KANAPOU

There is suggestion in the names around the island that Kahoʻolawe played a role in navigation to the ancestral lands to the south. The name of the channel between the island and Lānaʻi and the name of the westernmost point of Kahoʻolawe is Kealaikahiki, variously translated as "the way to the homeland", or "the way to Tahiti".

Kahoʻolawe was made a penal colony for men during the early 1800s. While the government ostensibly provided food for the prisoners here, it was not enough. Some prisoners swam to nearby Maui, where they stole food and canoes and returned to the island. Others took the Maui canoes and paddled to the dry northwest corner of Lānaʻi, where female prisoners were kept, and they escaped in couples to hiding places in the mountains of Maui. The penal colony on Kahoʻolawe was closed in 1853, and five years later a series of ranching ventures was launched.

Goats, sheep and cattle severely damaged the vegetation of the island, promoting the denuding of extensive areas and the erosion of the uplands. There were several efforts to control some or all of the grazing animals. By the time the military gained full control of the island for its bombing training, only goats remained. The goats were the first herbivores introduced to this island in 1793. After nearly two full centuries of munching, they were finally eradicated in the 1980s.

The island was returned by the federal government to the state in 1994, and is now overseen by the Kahoʻolawe Island Reserve Commission. The commission hopes to see the island cleaned up of ordnance, replanted in native vegetation and its marine resources protected. Eventually, it is seen as a potential center for Hawaiian cultural renewal.

Front cover Like a window to an older Hawai'i, Ke'anae peninsula offers views of taro ponds, banana groves and stately coconut palms. Waves crashing along the cliffs send a fine salt mist into the air.

Front cover Upper: Powerful ocean currents and blustering trade winds make Ho'okipa Beach a windsurfer's mecca.

Front cover Lower: Makena Beach is one of Maui's favorite isolated, end-of-the-road spots.

Back cover Upper left: South Africa's gift to Maui: protea blossoms transplanted to Kula in the 1960s and now cultivated Upcountry.

Back cover Upper right: Kiteboarding, or kitesurfing, has become a popular water sport widely recognized by its acrobatics, jumping, and flying.

Back cover Lower: One of Mākena's favorite beaches, secluded "Little Beach."

Page i Silversword at the summit of Haleakalā.

Page iii Horses and cattle on an upcountry ranch in Kula.

Page iv Sunset on Maui's Wailea Beach. Anglers, beachwalkers, and relaxation in a hammock slung between the coconut palms that curve over the sand, tinged pink-orange in the setting sun.

Page iv Sunset at Wailea Beach in front of The Grand Wailea Resort.

Page viii This waterfall on the Hanawī stream is accessible only from the ocean.

Page 2 Left: Kā'anapali's golden morning sand awaits the day's beachgoers.

Page 2 Above: Lokelani "The Maui Rose" is the official flower of the island of Maui.

Page 2 Right: A young girl in green aloha print sports a classic white and yellow plumeria lei during a hula performance.

Page 3 Late morning trades send a sailboat zipping past Kā'anapali's "Black Rock," home of the Sheraton Maui Hotel.

The site was once a sugar loading pier and, much earlier, a portal to the Hawaiian after life.

Page 4 Left: At Kaupō Ranch on the southern slopes of Haleakalā, a happy day on horseback under the Hawaiian sun.

Page 4 Right: The pink upright stalk and blossom of an ornamental variety of banana. This species is grown primarily for its appearance, not its flavor.

Page 5 Left: A pod of humpback whales travels through pristine Maui waters.

Page 5 Right: The islet of Molokini, lying between Maui and Kaho'olawe, is a tuff cone. Its side has eroded away, and the waters contained within the surviving crescent are protected as some of the best scenic diving reefs in the Islands.

Page 6 Left: Popular attire for a day outdoors in Hawai'i: a t-shirt printed in a Hawaiian theme and a bright bandana to protect the pate.

Page 6 Upper right: Kayaking is the best way to get into some of the remote bays and valleys of the Hāna coast.

Page 6 Lower right: Outrigger canoe practice happens at sunset almost every day at this, the main harbor of Moloka'i.

Page 7 Left: This plant grows in many of the valleys on the Hāna coast.

Page 7 Right: The opening ceremony of an annual festival in Hāna.

Page 8 This is the nightly torch lighting and cliff diving ceremony at the Sheraton Maui.

Page 9 Swimmers enjoy a Hāna waterfall trifecta at Waikani's "Three Bears" falls.

Page 10 Left: The Sheraton Maui anchors the Northwest end of Kā'anapali Beach.

Page 10 Above: A Hawaiian chanter leads in a hula halau for a performance in Hāna.

Page 10 Right: Tall, stately palm trees frame a Nāpili sunset.

Page 11 Lahaina's historic Front Street basks in a long, sunny West Maui afternoon.

Page 12 These trees, from Norfolk Island in the South Pacific, have been used extensively in the islands for re-forestation.

Page 13 Left: An early riser savors a flawless morning at Napili Bay.

Page 13 Right: At Kā'anapali, the sun may set in the palm of your hand.

Page 14 Yachts, fishing boats, dive tour craft and whale watching vessels in the afternoon sun line a section of the Lahaina harbor, as a rainbow climbs into the clouds in the background.

Page 16 Coconut palms cast a fringe of cool shade along azure Kapalua Bay.

Page 17 The massive Lahaina banyan provides shade for a collection of park benches. As it grows, the wide-spreading banyan provides its own support in the form of new trunks.

Page 18 Adventurers explore Kahekili's "olivine pools," named for flecks of greenish volcanic glass embedded there.

Page 19 Among the surf world's most coveted rides is the head-high, peerless right at Honolua Bay.

Page 20 Clouds, surf and a distant sail embellish a Kā'anapali sunset.

Page 22 Backed by championship golf courses, the Kā'anapali Resort wraps from Black Rock at left to "Canoe Beach" at far right.

Page 24 The tiny fishing and taro-growing village of Kahakuloa is protected by its jutting headland, which forms a stark, easily recognized landmark for those traveling to the sea on the west and north.

Page 26 The West Maui shoreline still shelters a few secluded "manager's houses" once used by sugar company executives.

Page 27 Majestic, Gibraltar-like "Elephant Rock" guards the old Hawaiian fishing and farming village of Kahakuloa.

Page 28 The view of Front Street in Lahaina from the sea, with a rainbow and the Pioneer Sugar mill smokestacks in the background.

Page 30 Left: School children enjoy an outing at Hawaii Nature Center in ʻĪao Valley.

Page 30 Above: Maui is the world capital of windsurfing and nowhere is more impressive, or dangerous, than the site known as Jaws.

Page 30 Right: Early window shoppers enjoy Pāʻia's sunny side while westbound commuters still have their lights on.

Page 31 The day's first windsurfers trace feathery signatures across Kanahā Beach Park's turquoise shallows.

Page 32 Left: An expert kite surfer blasts an aerial at Kanahā Park's "Kite Beach."

Page 32 Upper right: Outrigger canoe teams practice for the next regatta in choppy afternoon water off Kanaha Beach Park.

Page 32 Lower right: Maui Ocean Center which recently opened has proved to be very popular with both visitors and residents.

Page 33 Right: This roadside religious shrine is always well tended.

Page 34 Deep ʻĪao Valley is famous for its spire, the ʻĪao Needle, which is actually a point on a narrow, rugged ridge not far below Puʻu Kukui, one of the world's wettest spots.

Page 36 Offshore winds and powerful waves make Hoʻokipa Beach Park a proving ground for top board sailors worldwide.

Page 38 Sugar cane fields and Haleakalā volcano backdrop popular Baldwin Beach Park near Pāʻia.

Page 39 A rare windless morning sends straight aloft the towering ash and vapor cloud from a Central Maui cane fire.

Page 40 Truffle and mushroom vendors display their wares at the weekly Maui Swap Meet in Kahului.

Page 41 A youthful ʻukulele trio prepares to entertain First Friday festival-goers in Wailuku.

Page 42 Once humans leave the scene, the vegetation moves in quickly to reclaim the countryside. Banyans quickly begin covering old concrete and stonework, and their powerful roots will soon break apart solid rock walls.

Page 44 The north-facing coast of Central Maui includes some of the top windsurfing areas in the state. The old plantation village of Pāʻia, in the foreground, has become something of a boutique town catering to visitors and those engaging in active watersports.

Page 46 This commercial orchid farm near Wailuku is one of many that supplies flowers for everything from leis to tropical drinks.

Page 48 Left: Kahului is too tropical for regular apples but just right for juicy "mountain apples" like these at the Maui Nui Botanical Gardens.

Page 48 Right: Few tropical trees are as majestic and bountiful as the iconic, broad-leaved breadfruit, seen here at Kahului's Maui Nui Botanical Gardens.

Page 49 Left: ʻĪao Stream continues the work of ages: carving deep chasms in Puʻu Kukui, the ancient West Maui volcano. ʻĪao Valley's famous "Needle" rock is at center left.

Page 49 Right: ʻĪao Valley's cool, moist climate is ideal for torch gingers like this beauty at Tropical Gardens of Maui.

Page 50 Upper: The Kula Botanical Garden near Kēōkea raises colorful exotics like this pigtail anthurium.

Page 50 Left: Another Upcountry specialty is the "pincushion" or "sunburst" protea. These blooms are from Kula Botanical Garden.

Page 50 Right: This church in Kula is known for its distinctive octagonal shape. The interior is also very interesting.

Page 51 Cinder cones dot the interior of Haleakalā, whose dry weather and cold temperatures help prevent thick vegetation. Writers' favorite descriptive term for this region: lunar.

Page 52 Left: If you want cream puffs or doughnut holes on a stick from T. Kodama Store in Makawao, the line forms early.

Page 52 Upper right: What elsewhere would be a calendar photo is an everyday scene in Makawao.

Page 52 Below right: Among the hottest rides on Maui is the downhill run on bicycles from the summit of Haleakalā. Riders are fitted with helmets and the bikes have extra-sturdy brakes.

Page 53 Left: Once a cattle and dairy town, newly upscale Makawao maintains a rustic profile true to its origins.

Page 53 Right: Maui's historic ʻUlupalakua Ranch produces sheep, cattle, grapes and several popular wines.

Page 54 The stunning sunrises at Haleakalā require viewers to rise very early for the long drive to the summit, but provide outstanding views of cloud tops as well as the peaks of distant mountains on Hawaiʻi.

Page 56 Maui's Upcountry region is often brushed by passing clouds. Between the dry coast and the treeline is a wonderland of green pasture and tall trees.

Page 57 Brilliant purple jacaranda blossoms herald spring time on the slopes of Haleakalā.

Page 58 Narrow twisting Upcountry roads at Olinda, lined with bent fenceposts and postage-stamp kikuyu-grass pastures. Look down the sweeping slope of the volcano, and there's the sea.

Page 58 The Haleakalā silversword lives a quiet, silvery-spiky existence until it suddenly bursts into an amazement of bloom. Its myriad sunflower-like blossoms will seed, and then the plant will die.

Page 60 Among Hawaiʻi's signal wonders is Haleakalā National Park, a vast natural amphitheater of ragged cliffs, cinder cones, canyon lands and rain forests. The "Sliding Sands" hiking trail is visible at upper right.

Page 62 Haleakalā's 10,000-foot summit presents spectacular sunrises and sunsets in clear weather. It's hit or miss during rainy season.

Page 64 Upper: Palm trees become silhouettes as night falls on Mākena.

Page 64 Right: A former mayor's foresight preserved Kihei's pristine Kamaole beaches for public enjoyment in perpetuity.

Page 65 A quiet Sunday after church. Keawala'i Church at Mākena was built in 1832.

Page 66 Kama'ole Beach Park regularly draws sunset gazers hoping to see (and debate) the vaunted "green flash."

Page 67 Seen from Kīhei's Kamaole Beach Park on an exceptionally clear day, distant West Maui looks like a separate island.

Page 68 The 'Alalākeiki Channel glows orange, viewed through the branches of a coastal *kiawe* tree at 'Āhihi Bay.

Page 70 Hugging the South Maui shoreline is the world-class Wailea Resort, a galaxy of hotels, recreation facilities, restaurants and second homes.

Page 71 Many of Hawai'i's leeward resort golf courses are cut out of rocky regions thick with the thorny *kiawe*, seen at the top of this photo, a drought-tolerant tree imported as cattle feed. The coconut trees here are transplanted as mature trees. Besides providing cattle food, the *kiawe* is known for the flavor its charcoal imparts to barbecued food. Think mesquite.

Page 72 The distant slope of West Maui backdrops racing canoes beached at Kīhei's Maipoina'oeia'u Park.

Page 73 Kīhei palms frame a view of sunlit West Maui across Mā'alaea Bay.

Page 74 A classic Hawaiian scene, this Mākena area beach shot features manicured lawns shaded by coconut and *kiawe* and a sandy shore lined with *naupaka* and heliotrope. The hull to the left is Pu'u 'Ōla'i on Maui, and the island to the right is Kaho'olawe, with Molokini islet in front of it.

Page 76 The irrigated Wailea Golf Course thrives on the hot, sunny south side of Maui, and provides views of the 'Alalākeiki Channel and Kaho'olawe beyond.

Page 77 The sand channels are visible in the reefs within the old crater of Molokini, just three miles off the coast of Maui, and a favorite mooring spot for day diving charters.

Page 78 Afternoon clouds settle in over a Wailea Beach, where beachgoers are split between those who choose the sun and sand, and those who prefer covered beach chairs under the palms. The Grand Wailea and Four Seasons resorts are in the background.

Page 80 Afternoon trade winds set palm trees swaying at Mākena's Maluaka Beach.

Page 81 Castles built on the sand find their foundations threatened with each rising tide. Even protective seaward walls eventually are overwhelmed by the force of the waves.

Page 82 The flooded basins and low shrubbery of coastal wetlands provide habitat for a range of wildlife at Keālia Pond. Four endangered Hawaiian waterbirds, the stilt, coot, gallinule and duck, thrive in such habitats.

Page 84 Many Hawaiian families' beach houses of the early 1900s have been replaced by resort properties, but a few survive, as here are Kanahena, protected in part by the lack of sand on their shores.

Page 85 Sometimes there; sometimes gone. Tiny Pa'akō Beach is one of Mākena's surprise discoveries.

Page 86 The falling tide has erased all evidence of the footprints of the day's beachgoers, as the falling sun will erase the day.

Page 88 Big Beach aerial.

Page 90 Left: Hula dancer at Hāna festival.

Page 90 Above: Hāna Road. The road to Hāna with over 600 curves is considered the most scenic in Hawai'i.

Page 90 Right: Tutu's Snacks in Hāna Bay serves up shave ice and many other local style foods.

Page 91 Left: A young rider charges around the barrels in this

annual rodeo on the Hāna coast.

Page 91 Right: One of several fruit stands along the coast of Hāna.

Page 92 Once a private enclave for vacationing film stars, heiresses and CEOs, Hāna's sublime Hāmoa Beach today welcomes all comers.

Page 93 Fish are harvested annually from this pond in Hāna for celebration of a festival.

Page 94 Water has cut a path through different lava flows, but each erodes at a different rate, creating sudden drops. The result: waterfalls and cool pools. This is one of the lower pools at 'Ohe'o Gulch outside Hāna.

Page 96 The tradewinds and the seas that are driven before them have chopped away at the lavas of the windward side of Maui, creating small cliffs and large, and cutting out rugged bays.

Page 98 The coastal road swings in and out of one green valley after another: each alike; each distinctly different. Here, the Hāna road passes Honomanū Bay.

Page 100 Wailua falls is a popular stop between Hāna and seven pools.

Page 100 White-sand beaches made of ground coral and bits of shell are contrasted with rare black-sand beaches made of shards of basalt rock, created from the grinding of black rocks against each other on windward coastlines like the one below the road to Hāna, or in newer areas like the Kalapana Coast of the Big Island, from the breathtaking explosions of hot lava hitting the cold sea. This one is at Wai'ānapanapa State Park outside Hāna.

Page 102 Waterfalls plunge over the carpeted cliffs from a high rainforest watershed to the streams below. Some of these cliff faces, because they are inaccessible to grazing by goats, deer and cattle, are home to small communities of extremely rare native plants.

Page 103 Developing roads along the windward sides of the Hawaiian Islands is a difficult, often treacherous process because of deeply cut valleys, steep slopes and numerous stream channels. When successful, such roads meander snakelike through the terrain. Here, an aerial view of the Hāna Road.

Page 104 Lava rocks, hala trees and ocean waves make for a very rugged but beautiful coastline.

Page 106 Clouds mask the summit of cliffs that seem impossibly steep, as here at Manawainui Valley. While trees grow on these cliffs, they regularly become too heavy for shallow root systems that are unable to gain good footholds in the rock. The falling trees often launch rockslides that make the base of such cliffs dangerous places.

Page 107 Constant pounding of the sea creates jutting, tortured landscapes of rock peninsulas, sea stacks, caverns and arches. The Pauwalu Point, near the Ke'anae Peninsula on Maui's Hāna coast, is pictured.

Page 108 Kula lands, or plains, looking like something out of the old West, are often areas once covered by native dryland forest. Years of human use, involving fire and grazing, has replaced the dense forest with grassland. This scene is near Kaupō.

Page 110 Left: Plumeria, a very common flower in Hawai'i is known as frangipani elsewhere.

Page 110 Upper right: At the edge of the sea, boulders tumbled by the stream and rolled by the surf are rounded. These waters are alive with creatures like the 'o'opu, native gobies, which spend their early lives as plankton in the ocean, then return to the streams for an adult life in the cool, fresh water.

Page 110 Above: The rugged north coast of Moloka'i is a favorite of kayakers, but it is only accessible during summer. Winter surf pounds these coasts, making them hazardous for any kind of water craft.

Page 110 Right below: The Hula Piko is an annual festival held on the west end of Moloka'i.

Page 111 Left: The Moloka'i Mule Ride, from the top of the cliff down to and back from the Kalaupapa, peninsula is not as dangerous as it looks. However it is still not recommended for anyone afraid of heights.

Page 111 Right: This aerial view of the south coast shows clearly its fringing coral reef.

Page 112 Left: On rural Moloka'i, one of the unique activities available to visitors is the mule ride down a cliffside trail from Kala'e to Kalaupapa. The business has provided employment for cowboys in an age when cattle ranching is seldom profitable.

Page 112 Right: Hawai'i's longest stretch of sand is remote Pāpōhaku Beach, which runs for miles along Molokai's West End.

Page 113 Offspring of a king's plantation, leggy coconut palms tilt seaward from Moloka'i's storied Kapuāiwa Grove.

Page 114 The Mo'omomi dunes contain a unique Hawaiian sand dune ecosystem now protected as a wildlife refuge. The bones of ancient, extinct native birds have been found preserved in these sands, rare plants still grow here, and turtles haul up on the shores to lay their eggs.

Page 116 Moloka'i's Hālawa Valley, with Moa'ula Falls at its back, is often in shade. Its cliff walls are so steep that the sun enters only during the middle of the day.

Page 117 Horses graze in verdant tranquility at Moloka'i's scenic Kainalu Ranch.

Page 118 Afternoon clouds backlight Moloka'i's rugged northeast coast.

Page 120 Towering sentinel rocks like Huelo Island in foreground guard the world's loftiest ocean cliffs along Moloka'i's dramatic north shore.

Page 121 Also called "Father Damien's Church," Saint Philomena overlooks Moloka'i's scenic but tragic Kalaupapa Peninsula.

Page 122 Right, A former Hawaiian site on the east coast Kaunolū is now fairly inaccessible.

Page 122 Above: Golf holes extend to the edge of Lāna'i's southern cliffs. On Hole 12 of the Challenge Course at the Mānele Bay golf course, the grass is irrigated to maintain its green color. At the edges of the holes, the bare rock and dry grass reveals the normal arid condition of this region.

Page 122 Right below: Polihua Beach on the northwestern end of Lāna'i is famed in legend for its nesting turtles, which haul ashore here and lay eggs in the sand. The east end of Moloka'i lies directly upwind during most trade wind conditions.

Page 123 Drought-tolerant and colorful bougainvillea bushes frame the lawn and pool area of Lāna'i's Manele Bay Hotel, which overlooks the Mānele-Hulopo'e Marine Life Conservation Area.

Page 124 These petroglyphs are located just outside of Lāna'i City above old pineapple fields.

Page 124 Above: The central northern coast of Lāna'i is commonly known as Shipwreck Beach. Several wrecks have occurred on the reefs here, but the most visible today is this old freighter. Lāna'i lies downwind of the path of vessels passing through the Kalohi Channel on their way between Maui and O'ahu.

Page 125 Puhu Pe'e or "Sweetheart Rock" and the cliffs of Hulopo'e shelter Lāna'i's crescent-shaped Mānele Beach and its Four Seasons resort.

Page 126 Lāna'i City's famed Norfolk Island pines were planted years ago in an effort to trap the upland mists and increase the amount of moisture falling to the lee of the island's summit, Lāna'ihale.

Page 129 With Maui in the background, two sea stacks stand along the cliffs of Kaho'olawe, one of them attached to the island and one standing free. These stacks are among the few spots of this island whose native plants escaped destruction from the aggressive grazing by cattle, sheep and goats.

Page 130 Kanapou Bay on the east end of Kaho'olawe has one of the few beaches on the island.

Page 136 A pair of humpback whales cruise the sunset waters off Maui county, one taking a breather and the other displaying flukes. More than 2,000 humpbacks winter in Hawaiian waters each year.

'AU'AU CHANNEL